Where the Warehouse Things Are

,

Also by the Author

Lakas and the Manilatown Fish

Lakas and the Makibaka Hotel

BORN N' RAISED IN FRISCO: Words, Art and Resistance from a Colonized Displaced City Vol. 1

Cool Don't Live Here No More—A letter to San Francisco

Fingerprints of a Hunger Strike

Thrift Store Metamorphosis (Redhawk Publications, 2023)

WHERE THE WAREHOUSE THINGS ARE

A POETRY COLLECTION BY

TONY ROBLES

REDHAWK
PUBLICATIONS

WHERE THE WAREHOUSE THINGS ARE

ISBN: 978-1-959346-68-5 (Paperback)

Library of Congress Control Number: 2024945088

Any references to historical events, real people, or real places are used fictitiously. Names, characters, and places are products of the author's imagination.

Cover: Melanie Johnson Zimmermann

Book design: Robert T Canipe

Printed in the United States of America.

First printing edition 2024.

Redhawk Publications

The Catawba Valley Community College Press

2550 Hwy 70 SE

Hickory NC 28602

https://redhawkpublications.com

SCAN ME

Dedication

Hansel Robles

1935-2024

"He never got tested if there was anything in the warehouse, so to speak. If there was anything inside."

—Teddy Atlas

"Man is by instinct a lover, a hunter, a fighter, and none of those instincts are given much play at the warehouse!"

—Tennessee Williams

"IMAGINATION, n. A warehouse of facts, with poet and liar in joint ownership."

—Ambrose Bierce

"It's not only about money."

—Kaye Tefel

Contents

Introduction

A famous boxing trainer was analyzing a fighter's performance during a broadcast where he was facing his toughest opponent to date. It was a test of the up-and-coming pugilist's skill, fortitude, and courage—all the requisites needed to advance as a top-caliber fighter. *We'll see what he has in the warehouse,* the trainer remarked as the combatants plumbed the depths of the warehouses that stored their blood, spirit—fire. I thought of this while working at my current job at a warehouse in Hendersonville, NC. What was in *my* warehouse, I asked. I had never worked with tools; did not know a socket wrench from a toaster, a U-bolt from a U-boat. And there I was, under the bright lights of the warehouse, surrounded by a crowd of boxes and tools and implements, cheering, jeering, shouting: *Show us what you got*! I was told to make sure to secure bolts, to see to it that they were, as the German adage insisted (This is what the trickster techs told me), *goodintight.* In the warehouse, I was assigned the job of assembling motorized and manual wheelchairs and other accessibility items such as walkers and commodes. The bolts of anxiety and uncertainty were firmly placed in the warehouse that was me. As I worked assembling wheelchairs, I thought about the job with the display workers union in California, which I never showed up for, having been intimidated by the droves of men with staple guns in their holsters. I thought about another job that would have led to my becoming a merchant seaman. Again, I didn't show up after being intimidated by a hard-bitten seaman who was convinced

I smoked marijuana. Many years later, I find myself in a 15-round battle with myself in a warehouse in Western North Carolina. The warehouse is a chance to make good on my no-shows of the past. In building wheelchairs and commodes and walkers, I am, in a sense, building and repairing what was broken in me. I roll a cart filled with cardboard and refuse to a pair of metal debris boxes each morning and afternoon as part of my duties. I take the broken parts of myself and toss them into the boxes. I use the tools I've been given to build something new with new hands. I search the warehouse and find myself assembling and building what I didn't think possible. I come upon a box, a box that has been beyond my reach. I reach upward and finally pull it off the shelf. With my box cutter, I open it. It is filled with poems. It was what was in the warehouse all along. It is my gift to you.

Debris Box

Black bird

perched on a high

branch

Balance of sky

and wing as mountains

gather to keep warm

I push a cart filled with

cardboard and refuse to

a pair of metal debris boxes

at the bottom of small hill

The cart's wheels quiver

A concrete song,

treble set to

bits of pebble and glass

I open the large metal

debris boxes and the bird

laughs

Where the Warehouse Things Are

I visit the debris boxes

every morning, every afternoon

dumping the refuse

day by day

over and over

and the bird

laughs, again and

again

a schoolyard laugh

a faceless laugh

a laughter of stones

in a throat hollowed by years

I toss cardboard and trash

inside the rusted mouth

and remember the voices that

scratched at my insides

swallowing those sounds

like stones, hiss kindling in

my bones

And on this particular

trip to the metal debris box,

I haul those bones

and toss them into

the rusted mouth of metal

and rage

The mountains

silent

the bird

lifting in a strum

of mountain wind

I breathe in,

laugh

finally

Wrench of the earth

To wrench a poem from

between one's teeth while

working in a warehouse

using the wrench

as if a toothpick

is an act of genius

Wrenches have names

Crowfoot

socket

lug

dogbone

spoke

torque

impact

there's even one

named Allen

They are beginning to
fit comfortably in my
hand like a deck of cards
(Pick a wrench, any wrench)

The tool is conforming to me,
or am I conforming to it
I ask

Using a wrench
I remove a tumor
of uncertainty

And realize that
it is only the sun

Waiting to rise from
this warehouse
Wrenched from
Shadows

Warehouse

Warehouse with boxes

piled high blocking

the sun

Boxes stacked

like empires under the

weight of a fluorescent stare

I ask myself which box

I will check:

African-American

Filipino

55 or older

college grad

single

married

divorced

With a box cutter I cut

through boxes

Slicing upwards and downwards

and sideways

In a fish market in Japan

a man uses a long blade

to slice tuna

Slicing through the gleam

of blue skin as the eye

holds ocean's desperation

of salt

Slicing into sections

and chunks

An art handed down

through the current of centuries

I slice boxes in

a warehouse, boxes the

color of my skin

Where the Warehouse Things Are

Cutting away at the

boxes I have been put in

Like that man in

A fish market in Japan

Cutting towards art

Daylily Part II (For David)

In the warehouse a fan

circulates humid air

scattering scraps of paper,

moving across boxes,

containers of every

shape in search of skin

A warehouse breathes and

things grow under its

fluorescent glare

I assemble electric wheelchairs

and scooters, connecting wires

and joysticks and batteries

Bones and tendons shift

as I lock down, tighten

to specification using the

the proper tool to achieve

Where the Warehouse Things Are

maximum tension

All in an effort to help
someone move from point
A to B like a gust of humid air
free of tension

I am told to do a detail job
on a chair that has been
returned--a rental

I wipe a layer of dust from
it and my face comes into
focus

I look up and see another
Face, a man,
a very old man sitting in
the wheelchair

He reaches into his coat

pocket and pulls

something out

It is bright like fire and

I think of melted crayons

on the tips of my fingers

This is a daylily, the man

says. It only lives for one day

then it dies

The old man lies back in

the chair and hums a tune

that reminds me of butterscotch

candy

I'll be back, I say,

walking to the supply area

for this item or that

I return and find the

Where the Warehouse Things Are

old man is gone

In the wheelchair seat,
a daylily

It only lasts a day
then it dies

I take a hold of it
and let it live in my
skin as the humid air
of the warehouse moves
closer

Warehouse kind men

(For David, Suskey, James, Hornsby, Joe, Steve and Rob)

What kind men

in the warehouse?

Divorced kind men

fishing kind men

hunting kind men

Trouble shooting

kind men

Every tool in

the book kind men

Drills and bits and

pieces kind men

Top 40 hits from the

past, jazz and classical

and eclectic sounds from

lung's chambers kind men

Laughter like

confetti from their

Where the Warehouse Things Are

guts kind men

The kind of men that

say, well, that's not how

the world works as the

world tilts on its axis

Coloring the warehouse

beyond shades and shadows

of gray, beyond the pale

wearing lamp shades on

their heads kind men

Competent kind

men pushing past 50,

60 to the end of the

speedometer

kind men

Men who share

recipes, one of which is

drunken noodles

I can't seem to get

those noodles right, one

of the kind men says.

Maybe next time you

should cook them when

you're sober, another man

says

Warehouse kind men

The Girls Part I

Swollen with

Water the fragrance of

Crushed flowers

Swollen with

The dirt of her mother's

Grave

Cradled in a

Fingernail's curve

When passing in the

hall or shared walkway

she says, sorry

always mindful

always ready to defer

never to encroach

when in the warehouse

she looks at boxes stacked

high and standing side by

side like cemetery statues

a procession

a vigil of what

with swollen hands

she helps me piece together

a wheelchair, adjusting the wheels

to something called Hemi height

She shows me which

Tool to use

Her hands

Holding the sorrow of

The sweetest flower afloat

Tending the garden

Where the Warehouse Things Are

That is the warehouse

Pulling light from flowers

Trapped in boxes

shaping it with her

hands

Service call #1

The technician made me
nervous as we weaved through
the mountains in the company
truck

filled with tools awaiting
a glint of conversation
to cut through

The twists and turns
wove a gulf between us
that widened as the road
narrowed

a gulf of silence
interrupted by a
conservative radio talk
show host

The technician chewed
a piece of gum

In the hollow of my mouth
I form words misshapen

Words that die

Enroute to the tongue

The technician is a veteran

Was in Afghanistan.

Where the Warehouse Things Are

I have heard his laughter
at the warehouse

A laughter of stones held hostage

before skipping
across the face of water
towards freedom

before sinking

We both possess Spanish last
names that start with the
letter "R"

We sift through silence
as the road in front of us stretches
and the gulf of silence widens

The wind sweeps over us
a crescendo of words
stillborn

as we are
called to service

Pieces of a man

Drill bits boring

into what we think

we are

perhaps there are

holes in the

story

drills

probing

sounds wafting

in and out of

the warehouse

a wrench

a clamp

a screwdriver

ratchets

made to tighten

untighten

trying to keep

the pieces

Where the Warehouse Things Are

together

we build what

needs to be

built

and disassemble

what needs to be

discarded

and that drill

bit stirs in a frenzy

of torque

boring a hole

in the wall that

keeps

inviting our

eyes

to take a sip

of what's outside

the wall

Cardboard Paper cut

(For Suskey and James)

The technician

Cut the fuel line of

A bright orange car

A leak of profanities

Hit the warehouse floor

Pulp among

Oil splotches and spittle

The car destined to be sequestered

While the part ships in from

Korea

Another technician spews an

Expletive having opened a

Cardboard box containing a

Much needed part

Where the Warehouse Things Are

Shit, cardboard paper cut

He says, holding flesh to

The sear of white light

Both technicians

able, highly

Competent

Both not immune

Warehouse Veteran

In the warehouse

requisite symbols of military

prowess are on display

Flags from each branch of military

Stitched in silence

Rung with blood cursed hands

Hang from the rafters

One of the warehouse technicians

served in the army

His picture is on display

on a wall next to the customer

waiting area

In the picture he stands with

a rifle slung across his chest next

to a group of people in a village

Where the Warehouse Things Are

a world away

And his patience is on display as he

explains technical matters to laymen

having laid his weapons down

The earth of another part of

the world clings to the bottoms of

his feet

The air of a different land

filling his lungs

A quiet man

whose cell phone ringtone is

rapid bugle notes of a rapturous

reveille

A quiet man

who can't escape

the air, the earth of that other part

of the world

His laughter

comes out in rapid fire

reveille

an ambush

of riddles

Internee

We expected an old man
to arrive to pick up his
wife's wheelchair

I hadn't worked in the warehouse
very long and the others knew
the man, had remarked how
nice he was, especially the girls

He is so sweet,
they said

When he arrived at the warehouse
he stepped out of his mid-sized
American car

That's Mr. Sugimoto
a co-worker said

How old are you, Mr. Sugimoto,

someone asked

97 Mr. Sugimoto replied

He had a full head of hair
and didn't appear to carry any
excess in the middle

he stood waiting next to his
American made car in a parking
lot with a smattering of trees
shedding leaves

Autumn's shadow casting
an extended cameo

Somehow I knew

I remembered as a kid,
hearing about how one of my uncles
was mistaken for Japanese in the 40s
and was loaded onto a bus for the

Where the Warehouse Things Are

concentration camp

He was saved by my other uncle
who yelled to the authorities:
He ain't Japanese, he's Filipino!

In the ensuing years there have
been pilgrimages to those places
with names:

Poston

Manzanar

Tule Lake

Gila River

Jerome

Roher

Granada

Minindoka

Heart

Mountain

A warehouse of

memories

I look at Mr. Sugimoto

and out into the North Carolina

Mountains

Somehow I knew

Beautiful mountains, I say

Yes they are, he says

Both of us in

a moment of pilgrimage

What's your name? I ask

Ken, he says

Kenji

The Girls Part II

Brown-haired girl

of a thousand voices clenched

in laughter's fiery fist

Works in the warehouse

on the office side

Tattooed fingers weave

complex pattern formations

sweeping over parchment's

plainness

Hails from a hometown

population 420

tongue paved with

earth, sweet dirt where

420 varieties of flowers grow

where laughter sprouts

in moon's cuticle of complexity

and equations of arcs in

unequaled eloquence

Speaks with a thousand

small town voices for which

there are no caricatures

A post office stands alone

in her hometown of 420

sealed in stoic silence

Awaiting a letter

from a brown-haired girl

Warehouse Leaf Blower

Fog horns

bellow symphonies

Beneath breath

Of stars

Leaves are

Blown across concrete

        Off course

leaves

of every color

tumbling like starfish

Seeking escape

To Satchmo's

Lips

       Of course

Leaf blower

blowing

a blasphemous

tune

peace

disrupted

as if

extinguishing

a

poem

From

a

Page

Warehouse Radio

A song fights its way

through the speakers

A song from the past

that holds meaning

But to the warehouse its

just another voice coming

through wires and speakers

A familiar song that knows

me and I, it

It knows me the way the

warehouse doesn't

A secret song

Only I hear it as the crew of

Warehouse workers convene

I struggle to hear my song

Over the voices

To be interrupted

by a sermon of a forklift

scraping concrete

Warehouse Back Scratcher

It stands upward

shooting from a cup on my

desk like a riding crop

the warehouse cat

has crept near my foot

its claws dig into

the cobalt carpet

plucking with and against

the grain

an itch inches its way

up my back like the silken

fingers of cornstalk

the cat looks up

at me

only she

can scratch

this itch

Paperback

Working in a warehouse there's

a radio blaring hits

of yesteryear

pallets of merchandise

come through the loading dock

like long lost ships

The radio provides a sound

track as we track each item

by packing slip, serial number

One song moves towards me, a tune

called Paperback Writer

I am a writer working

in a warehouse

A warehouse of thought,

of laughter, of emotion

Where the Warehouse Things Are

and sudden expletives captured

by a forklift a mouthful at a time

How many writers

work in warehouses?

How many stories are

on the shelves waiting?

How many poems are

collected by the dust mop, sweeping

across floor's memory?

I sit and wait but not for long

as there is always something

stirring

Wanting to be a paperback

writer, writing on the back of napkins,

a slab of cardboard, the back of my

hand

How many writers work

in warehouses waiting for a story

to inch its way through the loading

dock and slap them with the back

of its hand?

Pallet

Stage of

splinters and nails

Platform of suns

packaged by sons

A harvest of

boxes through interstate's

busy arteries

Pallet

a stage where drivers

stand under blue veined

skies reciting lyrics

carved into packing slips

With splintered tongues

They recite sacred words

"Hey buddy, got a big

one for you today."

Moving from one warehouse

engagement to the next

before standing room only

audiences of boxes and

shelves and forklifts

And with a voice

big like the sky

Steps on the pallet,

clears the throat

sings a song

of splinters, nails

packing slips

Hitting notes

just right, nailing it

Before moving on

to the next venue

Warehouse Part II

The boxing trainer turned TV

boxing analyst watched an up

and coming fighter absorb much

punishment, behind on all scorecards

going into the middle rounds

It was a test of the fighter's courage,

fortitude, heart

We're going to see what

he has in the warehouse, the trainer

turned analyst remarked

I thought of this at my job working

in a warehouse

Walking underneath fluorescent

lights before an audience of

cardboard boxes of all sizes

storing cheers, boos, hisses,

near misses and other surprises

Every tool, drill and bit calls this

Warehouse home as well as jacks

and hitches

This is a home of tools with

names I can barely pronounce

I look in warehouse boxes,

one is labeled strength, another,

courage, another perseverance

I open the boxes

and find they are empty

Another box with no label sits

alone on a nearby shelf

I open it

Inside are arms, legs, a torso,

Where the Warehouse Things Are

a face that looks much like mine

I take each part from the box

and try to piece it all together

into something that looks like:

courage

heart

fortitude

As I find out what's inside

the warehouse

Fork Lift

I looked at the forklift

in the warehouse at a

distance that covered

the space between the

words can and can't

The forklift looked at

me and asked, do you want

to take a stab at it?

The forklift is big and

loomed over me and I felt

like I was back in grade

school again

Two big prongs that

protrude, ready to slide

into pallets

Sometimes breaking them,

leaving behind splinters

but emerging unsplintered

I think of my father,

Where the Warehouse Things Are

a working man who made it

possible for me to lift a fork

to my mouth

I stabbed at food with

fork that my father

had provided

And sometimes he put

down his fork and ate

with his hands, thick brown

hands like a true Filipino

And the forklift

stands across from me

in the warehouse

waiting for me to

take a stab at it.

Warehouse Hex

Perhaps it

was a hex

Never built up

enough calluses

to rid myself of it

Never good with my

hands was what the palm

reader said before thrusting

her palm towards me

I could have slapped myself

for laying 30 dollars on her

palm for telling me what I

already knew

In the warehouse I'm

the new guy

They handed me a cluster

of metal pegs

What's this? I asked

An Allen wrench, they

Where the Warehouse Things Are

answered, you'll need

it

I never seemed to fit

in at work or in other

places

The Allen wrench

is made of metal

and comes in many

sizes

I'm told to assemble

an electric wheelchair

I take the Allen wrench

and after a bit of struggle

manage to put the wheelchair

together

The Allen wrench

has found a home in

my hand,

it fits

Hex

Broken

Assembling a Wheelchair

Some assembly

required the directions

say

Yet our right to assemble

has been under attack

So many broken humans

among us

Yet the sun still

breaks through clouds

And in a warehouse, a poet

who could barely tie his

shoelaces manages to

assemble a wheelchair

Moving parts meeting static

Where the Warehouse Things Are

ones, wheels with spokes whose

sounds are never misspoken

yet move in

every direction

And somewhere a wheel chair

is being put together while a

world tilts on its axis trying to

find its bearings

Every part

important to the

movement

like an arm

connects to torso

like tendons

like heart

and mind

all connected

part of one movement

Laid to rest

At the warehouse where I work

the light comes through at

different spots

Through windows

The garage door

Through gaps underneath

doors

The glare of florescent lights

hits my eyes and I have gotten

used to it as I have gotten used

to non-fat milk

In prisons across the world

people wait to see daylight

while others have given up

that hope

Where the Warehouse Things Are

And in the warehouse,

I disinfect mattresses

Some smooth, some lumpy,

some sunken, taking on the

shape of those who have lain

on them

And a mattress comes back from the VA,

blue and wide and I think of an

aircraft carrier even though I've never

been on one

I am told

the man who had it

recently died

I take the mattress, spray it with

disinfectant and scrub it under the

watchful fluorescent light

I leave it to dry,

and return 30 minutes later

On the mattress is an old man

whose eyes search my face while

my eyes search his

"How you doin' pop?" I ask

"I'm ready to go to a better

Place", he answers," or maybe

a worse one"

"Help me up"

I take a hold of the man's arm

and pull him to his feet

"Hand me my shirt and pants"

He dresses himself and

asks, where's my tie?

Where the Warehouse Things Are

In your pocket, maybe, I say

And he ties his tie as if he's

getting ready for the senior prom

"This way, sir", I say

And the man walks towards the

garage door and the light hits him

and now he is young

"Where are you going?' I ask

To the prom he says, smiling

He walks away and I watch

until he disappears

I close the warehouse door

and walk back to the cleaning

station to disinfect another bed

from the VA.

Sewing

The mattresses at the warehouse

sit stacked like slices of

Texas toast

They require an air pump

so the veterans that sleep

on them can breathe easily

I wipe down the mattresses

when they come back from

the VA

Stained with dreams,

nightmares

in the shapes of

people, countries

I wipe back and forth

with a large sponge with

Where the Warehouse Things Are

disinfectant in its pores

I notice a tear in the seam

and someone asks, do you know

how to sew?

I am given a needle

and thread, pull up my

shirt and see an open

wound

A gaping mouth

festering in doubt,

insecurity

I've never sewn before

but you learn new things

about old things and I see

my wound with new eyes

I finally sew

the wound shut

And pack the mattress

in plastic

Ready to be shipped

to a destination to absorb

dreams, nightmares

again

Pallets

(After Oscar Penaranda)

Pallets rise and fall on

forked tongues with fingerprints

Lifted, stamped with names, tracking

numbers, serial numbers under

the glare of warehouse lights

the color of

fat-stripped milk

My palate is

a silent symphony

half swallowed

The warehouse

is palatial as far as

pallets are concerned

Boxes sit throne-like

atop pallets stacked alongside

more pallets

Boxes stacked in a citadel

of a silent chorus

Some crushed

some looming higher

The pallet is a splintered

stage holding boxes of

dreams

some crushed

some damaged

Handle with care

Open Heart

Electric wheelchairs are

brought in for maintenance

Parts need to be replaced

Do trees have artificial

limbs?

In the warehouse

the wheelchairs sit and

await repair

Each one has a

ticket with a name

written on it

And a man brings an

electric wheelchair to the

warehouse

He needs help lifting

it

I just had open heart,

he says, touching the

Shirt seam above his

Chest

We take the wheelchair

from the bed of his

pickup

and the man's wife sits

in the truck

On the dashboard is

a red pillow in the

shape of a heart

The wheelchair is

for me, she says

Where the Warehouse Things Are

And in that truck I

feel love that is shared

by a husband and wife

a beautiful thing

like an open heart

Forked

My uncle used to listen to an
old song on a scratchy record
called "A Fork in the road"

The lyrics told of the dangers that
lie ahead and he'd sing along
with the record, the lyrics
washing over him

Reminding him of some
wrong turn in love's interstate
where he found himself without
a map

I think of him while working a fork lift
at a new job in a warehouse filled
with electric and manual wheelchairs

Where the Warehouse Things Are

Removing a pallet with the forklift,

I uncover a snake that has been crushed,

its head smashed, a drop of blood

oozing

The snake slithers, coils and

recoils

My co-workers are not snakes

(At least I think they aren't)

and they gather around looking

at the snake

One of them scoops it up with a

slice of cardboard

That was a beautiful snake,

they say in silence before going

back to work

Men like these

do not speak

with forked tongues

Where the Warehouse Things Are Part I

Enter the warehouse

was like Enter the Dragon

but instead of martial artists

I found myself surrounded by

technicians whose hands held

the riddle of how-to wisdom

and knowledge

I was never good with my hands in

terms of mechanical things and I was

in awe of guys who knew how to fix

things or put things together with

their hands or teeth (or both)

Guys like these seemed to use pliers,

screwdrivers and wrenches at the

dinner table while I used an ordinary

knife and fork

Where the Warehouse Things Are

The warehouse door opened
and there they stood

Don't be afraid,
the one with the long grayish
beard said

I stepped past the garage
threshold and onto a concrete
floor that gave off a smooth
sheen

"Wait, I recognize you", the balding
one with much facial stubble
said

"You were with the display union
but you never showed up"

It was true, I joined but never
showed up after seeing all those

guys with tool belts equipped

with staple guns ready to aim at me

That was 3000 miles away and

40 years ago, how the hell did

this guy know?

"What have you been doing the

last 40 years", they asked

"Writing", I replied

"To who, the parole board?"

I've never been arrested.

"Yeah, he looks pretty soft"

the one with the southern

drawl remarked

We stood looking at

each other

Where the Warehouse Things Are

It's been 40 years since I've

set foot in a warehouse

"Let's get started", the men say

And I follow their trail,

a dot at the bottom of a

question mark

with 40 years' experience

behind me

Where the Warehouse things are Part II

(For Joe, David and Rob)

We gathered at the other

warehouse a short distance

from the main warehouse.

The other warehouse where a

glitter of glorious rust had settled in the

toilet and where inventory is piled

and stacked in corners, on pallets;

hitches, hospital bed frames,

elevated toilet seats and various

spare parts

We met there,

a technician, a delivery driver

and 2 warehouse workers

We gathered to learn how to

assemble a bed piece by

piece

Where the Warehouse Things Are

A bed made specifically.

for children prone to self-

inflicted injuries

Down Syndrome

Autism

The technician showing us

how to assemble is a big man,

6 foot 4 or 5, 300 plus pounds

of football prowess before breaking

his leg in a college all-star game

piece by piece

bolt by bolt

screw by screw

we assemble the wood

parts, the metal parts, the

glass

the big man is

a patient teacher

"Hey, you get in on

this too", he said to me

and I lifted part of the bed

frame, sliding the bolt into the

correct hole.

"You know, my father never

showed me how to do nothin'",

one of the guys says

"That's why I got to pay

someone whenever I need

to get anything done".

Another fellow said, "yeah,

my father would show me how

to do something, only he would

do it himself and I'd sit and watch

like a dummy"

Where the Warehouse Things Are

And I thought of my father

and saw that he was like

their fathers.

But I still

love him

And we got that

bed assembled

all of us, together,

butting heads with

the memory of our

fathers

assembling a

bed made for children

prone to self-inflicted injuries

putting it together

                together

with all the care built in the

callous nature of our hands

some of us, fathers

Not wanting to

see a child

hurt themselves

Warehouse Sonnet #1

Warehouse tongues sharpened by the wit of knaves

Light sucked through straws of phosphorescence

Hammers igniting silent cadence of thought

Hands clutch tools bending prayers into alloy's folly

Brain constellations traced on a warehouse wall

Shadows conform to misshapen dreams of flesh

Matters of brain a tool belt question mark

Couriers bring news on cardboard walls.

Tools lift fingerprints as evidence.

It's a man's job but a woman births it.

Cardboard mansions rise in perfumes of dust

A pallet is a stage of splintered cargo.

A hand truck declares a strike starts a movement.

Tools affix names to the heart's remnants.

Warehouse Cat

A cat appeared at the
warehouse with eyes the
color of everything I couldn't
see

A cat from the streets
A homeless cat

calloused paws

I've never been homeless

It came in as if it were its
first day of work and
immediately took a break

Light lift of paw
easing into the in-between
spaces of this place, settling

Where the Warehouse Things Are

between two bulky

boxes sitting on a metallic shelf

I watch the cat as if it were a

shadow from a mime's mirror

before going back to assembling

manual and motorized wheelchairs

The cat leaps from the shelf and

smoothes its coat, its body across

surfaces of boxes, wheelchairs,

regular chairs

my ankle

Leaving traces of

grace on the sum parts of

both body and machine

I continue to work,

limbs contorting, conforming to

limited ranges of motion

As the cat moves,

light of limb

towards me

casting elegance

in a warehouse of

eyes

the wind's season of

argument

now a purr

No Gold Watch

An old man stopped

by the warehouse looking

for a new cane

He entered the showroom

floor and browsed the

different types of canes

Some had 1 rubber tip,

some had 4

(A "quad" cane)

He opted for the single

tip but he wanted to keep

the tip of his old cane

The tip is known as a

ferrule--pronounced like

feral, as in cat

The lady from the showroom

floor brought me the man's old

cane, asked me to remove the old

ferrule

It was a bit worn but

still in good shape as I

grabbed it and pulled and

found that it was stubbornly

in place

I pulled harder and the

ferrule seemed to grip my

hand, putting its indention

into my skin

I've walked many miles, seen

many places, poked my way

across the earth the cane

seemed to say

I worked it, twisting clockwise,

counter-clockwise until

removing it like a cork from a

champagne bottle

The lady took it to

the man who was waiting on

the showroom floor

5 minutes later she

Where the Warehouse Things Are

returned with a gold cane

What's this? I asked

The old man says

you can have it

I took the cane and placed

it gently against the

warehouse shelf

Where it will wait

to prop up the sun

and the moon

and someday

maybe me

Cutting Cardboard in a Warehouse

They give you a pair

of box cutters

and the deliveries

never end

Couriers in and out

dropping off cardboard

boxes

The workers pull out the

parts, electronic entrails

leaving only cardboard rinds

Some boxes go unopened,

left to sit on pallets

I cut the cardboard

skin, slicing upwards and

downwards and I think of

Where the Warehouse Things Are

the way my grandmother cut

lechon

I think of the unhoused people

back home whose prayers were

scribbled on cardboard

"Please Help"

"Homeless and hungry"

god bless

And in the warehouse

the cardboard boxes pile up

and on the warehouse radio is

an old song called Sunshine

of your love

And I cut

and slash through the

cardboard toward light

Warehouse Philosopher

In the warehouse the deliveries

come in by way of big trucks and

couriers who are at times

diminutive

Some look like jockeys

whose legs might dangle

from the seats of their cabins

Upbeat and cheerful

they are, writing notes on

delivery slips and fanning

themselves with dented

clipboards

The license plates read

Tennessee, Virginia, South

Carolina and other places I

have never been

A delivery of commodes

Has come in, an important

commodity requiring

Where the Warehouse Things Are

Some assembly

Never being mechanically inclined,

I rise from my reclining position

and sign for the commodes while

putting on my philosopher's cap,

transforming into the philosopher

Albert Commode

And I read the directions on how

to assemble a "Drop arm commode"

knowing that I have the right to

assemble and I put it together one

piece at a time

The last thing I

want to drop in this commode

is an arm (especially mine)

I take up arms with

The not so clearly written

Instructions in hand

And with that

Albert carries the commode

to the sales floor

Ask the Dust Mop

The dust mop leans against the

warehouse wall

watching

It has moved across the

warehouse floor

back and forth

Turning at this angle

or that

Getting into hard to reach

areas and moving into a

holding pattern at times

before leaning against the

warehouse wall, observing

The dust mop tells me

that we are all going back

and forth and eventually back

Where the Warehouse Things Are

to the dust from where we come

And I think of a great writer who

wrote a book called, Ask the Dust

And like that writer, I too

am a dreamer

I occupy the area

between dust and dreams,

my fingers stained with both

Ready to push the dust mop

across the floor

in a warehouse

in Western North Carolina

The Boss

(For Kaye)

Lips that sing

Biblical passages of

Prophets

Slight twang

Of voice

Wink in the eye

That recalls the brilliance

Of a night star

In the morning

Or afternoon

Or in the

Fall of night

Full flight

A face filled with

Memories of a mother

Where the Warehouse Things Are

Who cooked potato soup

Didn't grow up with money
But with faith and potato soup
And home stitched shirts and
Dresses

And she brings us together
From the warehouse to her
Table

Filled with songs and food
And directives

Safe passage

Slight twang from
Strings stitched into
The fabric of a warehouse

Joined together
Like home-stitched shirts,
dresses

Benched

Working in the warehouse

surrounded by drills

and batteries and shelves

Tools in their

tool drawers and

toolboxes

I'm getting used to

the drill

I am given an assignment,

put together a bench

I cut the cardboard box,

slicing into it like a holiday ham

or Filipino roast pig like my uncle

used to do back home

Where the Warehouse Things Are

The wood slabs

lie in a box in wrapping paper

and as I unwrap them, I see the

horizontal direction of the grain

I think about a splintery bench

I once sat on, the wood untreated

while on the Jr. Varsity football team

in high school

I was cut from the team

before my cleats could be

broken into

But not before taking part in

a fumble recovery drill where I

recovered the ball and eluded the

tackle of a player with an extremely

hideous face

I knew the drill

And now I put together a bench

in a warehouse and a kid

sits on it, a kid of about 15 or

so

He's wearing a football

Uniform, fresh cleats

The wood is splintered,

untreated

We sit together

Huddled in a life of fumbles

splinters

Warehouse Tongue Twister

(For JH)

Learning how to remove and install

batteries in electric wheelchairs

and scooters

volts, amps

an array of sizes

and serial numbers

and grounding cables

See if you can pull it

out, a technician tells

me with the smile

of a dentist

I am a warehouse rookie

who once had 6 wisdom teeth

removed while awake

I manage to pull out the

battery, extricating it

from a tangle of cables

There are some batteries

that are housed in a casing

that require the removal of

screws

With a drill-like tool

he removes it

"Don't strip the screw head"

he warns

And I repeat the words

in my head, trying to savor

its wisdom spoken through

technical teeth

Don't strip the screwhead

Don't strip the screwhead

don't scrip...strip the

screwhead

Don't scrip the

strew head

No, don't

mis-con-strew

Don't

screw

Where the Warehouse Things Are

I mean

con-strue

I mean,

just screw

the damn

thing on!

Pronation and Supination

Uncle Anthony used to come

around, once, twice, three

times a week

He wore shades

whose lenses were sometimes

red, sometimes blue and

sometimes yellow

the color

the seasons of

his life

He wore a black leather

coat like a panther and inhaled

music and kept it in his bones

He could laugh into the sky

and make it rain

flowers

Where the Warehouse Things Are

He would look down

at me, his nephew that

bore his name

Slap me five, he'd say,

offering me his palm

I'd slap it and

then he'd say, on the

black hand side

And I'd slap the backside

of his hand with the backside

of mine, his skin giving off all

the black and brown of his life

And my hands that touched

my uncle's and all the skin he

had in the game to give, are now

used to work a screwdriver, Allen

wrench and other tools in a

warehouse

And I've learned that palms downward

is called pronation and palms upward is

called supination

I turn the bolts and screws, hands

in pronation or supination depending

on what's needed

But it

can't drown out the

words of my uncle years ago

Slap me five

On the black hand side!

Full Circle

My father had every jazz

album ever recorded

or so it seemed

the album covers

sat at different angles like the

brim of a hat as the music drifted

and wafted through every room of

our landlord's flat

rent was 450.00 a month

and my father worked as a janitor

to cover it as well as food in my

gut, clothes on my back

According to him, I was

proficient at 3 things:

1. eat

2. sleep

3. shit

And he'd play his jazz records,

laying them on the turntable that

turned like a combination lock, allowing

him a kind of entrance I didn't

understand

to me, it was just some guy

blowing air into a horn

I tuned most of it

out

those records turned clockwise,

the sounds returning like Karma

A coworker once told me,

Where the Warehouse Things Are

righty tighty, lefty loosey

and 3000 miles away
working in a warehouse, I lie on my
back trying to screw a bolt into a
power wheelchair

righty tighty

But I am turning too
hard and strip the threads
to the bolt

I remember my father's jazz
records and how they turned
clockwise

Those great records:

Giant steps
Milestones

Now is the time

Above the warehouse

a bird hovers and

calls out

And what has been

stripped has returned,

threads of sound coming

full circle

as the music wafts

and drifts among the looming

mountains and into a warehouse

where karma turns

and turns like a bolt

3000 miles away

in North Carolina

All Of Me

Sometimes a song sneaks in

through the vents, the pipes,

under the warehouse door

When it comes

it quiets everything

the drills no longer make

drilling sounds, the hydraulic

lifts give a hiss before surrendering

to gravity

the songs of machinery

come to a halt

The vice has loosened

its grip

And the words, *All of Me*

come, soothing its way

towards me

an old standard

from a well-oiled

throat

Unpinching a nerve

that has left me unnerved

ending all interruptions

All of me, why not take all of me?

Can't you see I'm no good without you

The song soothes me

and I know I have to work

like I've worked many jobs

But I can't give

all of me

to a job

Only a poem

Pushcart

The parts of a manual wheelchair

sit stuffed in a warehouse box

waiting for the assembly of my

hands

a dermis of

disarray and deficits

of derelict DNA

Webs of occasional

misdeeds

Touch the cool skeletal

of each part

Elevated leg raises

anti-tippers

brake levers

foot rests

arm rests

Push rim

My hands touch

each part as if it

had a soul

and I wonder if

God takes the fingerprints

of faith healers

A minor miracle, I fully assemble it

And push it

to the sales floor where someone

will sit on it, someone like 94-year-old

Mrs. Sugimoto whose husband Ken will

deliver

Who will move towards

mountains in the morning

Where the Warehouse Things Are

Easing into another season

like a snow crane swimming in sky

Pulling the sun

staining the sky

while a newly hired

warehouse apprentice

is pushed

towards poetry

Daydream

In the warehouse

there are portals where light

leaks through

Porous openings in patches of

glass, a small hole where a congregation

of rust has spread like a sore

Light is persistent and my eyes

seek it as it takes a hold of

my daydreams

Daydreams got me

in trouble

My eyes danced and darted

and bounced off the classroom

walls in the direction of the window

Where the Warehouse Things Are

I was kept after school for the

daydreams that were more dust

than chalk

I look out the window

of my job at the warehouse

In the sky are two birds, one with

a wingspan of about 6 feet while the

other is a bit smaller

Fluttering in cursive, dipping and

swerving over territory or perhaps

just playful jostling

There's work to be done, can't

spend all day gazing at the sky

My eyes follow the movement

of the birds as they call out: Don't stop dreaming

Warehouse Romance

I was told never to talk

about

Politics &

Religion

And never date

anyone at work

advice I followed religiously

She came in through the void

of a vent

Nobody heard her

Carl Sandburg wrote of fog

coming in silently on cat feet

Where the Warehouse Things Are

She came in through the vent

or was it the front door?

Over the loud speakers

of the warehouse is a song

called American Woman

Her coat was gray with

stripes that whipped across

my mind

Green eyes that

could still an emerald

sea

She brushed against me

leaving a fragrance of

questions

Are you harassing me,

I asked

She purred and leaped towards

something resembling the moon

and my eyes followed and my work

in the warehouse began to suffer

I kept working, recalling the sexual

harassment videos I was forced to

watch upon being hired

She lingers

brushing against my leg

leaving behind a purr

No longer able to endure the

harassment

I take the cat

Home

Warehouse Constellation

Toolbox filled

with clichés whose

pronouncements

lie prone

screw driver

pliers

hammer

wrench

Names formed

by torqued tongue

dust settles on my

poet's eye

as tools seek hands that

speak toil's calloused

dialect

Toolbox, a coffin

of pent-up ranges

of motion seeking

a mission

torque

tension

loosen

release

They speak, asking,

what's your name?

I give it but there

are tools whose names

I do not know

hex key

prey bar

A technician raises a car on

an "above ground lift"

hoisting its offering to the gods

He traces his fingers across the

underbelly over constellations

of metallic braille sharp to the

touch

I'm the new guy in

the warehouse, watching as the

technician loosens bolts and

Where the Warehouse Things Are

screws

My poet's eye slides upward to

a cache of stars

Hey, hold this

the technician says placing

a bolt in my hand, rusted

A star

Hand me a wrench,

he says

as the calluses form

Catwalk

She was a jolt from

nowhere yet from everywhere

and the music of her form

was the seductive notes of

midnight jazz and her steps

were pinpoints of light in

an inky black sky, legs stretching,

bending notes, in measured

movements incalculable to the

equations of man

From nowhere she walked

into the warehouse where

inventory is taken, counting

wheelchairs, canes, commodes

and other commodities but not

counting on this green-eyed

tabby to enter this stage of

fluorescent light adorned in

stripes and preparing us

for opening night

Open Door

In the warehouse the heat
and cold travel throughout
in patterns not visible to the
eye yet felt in the pores

one door says:
"Keep this Door
Closed at All Times"

but the door somehow opens,
it is ajar to be opened and closed
again and again

It is an effort to conserve
heat we are told

Nobody knows who keeps
opening the door

all mouths are closed
except one, Steve's

Speaks with what would
be called a country accent

When I hear it I think of
old western TV shows
molasses and sourwood honey
dripping from the corner of a
mouth coming to a halt

Steve speaks:
"It's been a year today
since Mama passed"

and the warehouse door
is shut as it is supposed to be

Steve continues:
"I closed the door to Mama's room
last night and this morning it
was open"

Maybe it's the wind, or maybe

Where the Warehouse Things Are

it was your dog, a coworker says

Steve shakes his head, no,
it definitely ain't that

We shake our heads
pondering while the warehouse door
opens

it is mama
telling us: Keep it open

your heart
your mind
your love
your ability to forgive

Why?

Because I'm Mama
and I said so...

Uncivilized

My father would eat with his

Hands across from me at the

Kitchen table

in the true Filipino way

He'd scoop the rice and tomatoes

And chilis and tuna and it would

Stick to his fingertips

He would swallow question

Marks, exclamation points and

Belch musical notes that only

He could hear

He chewed and chewed

And I sat with my fork,

Not knowing why he ate

With his hands

I told a friend and he told

His father and his father

Said that my father was

Uncivilized

Where the Warehouse Things Are

And my father would look

At me from across the kitchen

Table and say, if you want anything

In this life, you got to get off your

Ass and work for it

Ain't nobody gonna give you

Nothin' for free, he'd say, the

Rice grains sticking to the side

Of his mouth

Now get off your ass and wash the

Dishes

I work in a warehouse now, several

Decades later and I operate a

Forklift

And I put down that forklift

At 5pm and when I get home

I eat with my hands

Swallowing question marks,

Exclamations points, trying to

Digest the main points and pointless

Aspects of my life

Belching musical notes while

Eating with my hands

Anything less

Would be uncivilized

Lion Trainer

(For Joe)

When the lion is a

trainer, he doesn't

use a stick or a whip

There's no 3 ring

circus with cotton candy

popcorn hot dogs

A ring of fire is his

his training ground

he comes with knowledge

and pride

In a warehouse he plies his

trade piecing together machinery

bit by bit, part by part

If there's no manual

or written instructions

he figures it out by instinct

The lion's voice is

husky having swallowed

a lifetime's worth of

honey and fire and

earth and salt

In the grip of his

jaw he holds patience

and the delicate stems

of dandelions

An easy smile but his

eyes are that

of a lion

a trainer

A big, good-natured

teddy bear to those

around him

Make no

mistake, he's

a lion

It's in his skin

it's in him

A lion whose roar

lives in a

warehouse

Don't play

with a lion

Tenderly

Turning the screws clockwise

removing bolts counterclockwise

Adjusting the height

of a wheelchair

Affixing the brake levers

the anti-tippers

Making sure the armrests

are set at the proper width

Assembling everything

properly, bolted into place,

screwed down tight

It's a man's work

in this warehouse

working with hands

But the moon above the

warehouse sits, how high

I do not know

Show me the music

of your hands, it

says

And I listen for the sound

of my fingers, tendons,

callouses

I tighten the bolts

                tenderly

affix the

old metal parts

                tenderly

turn the screwdriver,

the Allen wrench

                tenderly

Who knew you

could be tender in a

warehouse of cold parts

looking for the warmth of

touch?

Maybe the moon

Maybe the man whose

legs no longer

move as they once did

but whose eyes move

Where the Warehouse Things Are

towards you speaking

the words, thank you

        tenderly

You have to move forward, son

Pushing a garbage cart

towards a pair of metal

dumpsters at the foot of a

small hill paved in tears of

concrete

Wheels rumble over

pebbles and bits of glass

A music of movement

in bits and pieces

The mountains that surround

this space rumble in silence

a mountain of hunger

the mountains feed me

its beautiful silence

beautiful edges

Where the Warehouse Things Are

jagged poems sprouting

everywhere

My father's voice cuts

through the silence

from 3000 miles away

You have to move forward

in life, son, he says

I push a garbage cart

over the pebbles and

stones that have washed on

the shore of my life

The cutting edges

leave its traces as I pluck

a few and place into my pocket

I toss a few stones

towards the mountain

I move forward towards

the metal dumpsters

discard what needs

to be discarded

drawing a breath of

mountain silence

moving forward

Warehouse Clock

The clock in the warehouse

dropped from the wall

and crashed to the floor

Its innards were intact

yet its arms were immobile,

frozen at 320pm

The second hand was

stuck at quarter to the

hour

I lifted the clock

from the floor

I'd looked at its face

many times while working at

this warehouse piecing together

manual and electric wheelchairs,

commodes, elevated toilet seats

and other such devices

I lifted the clock,

coming face to face when

it spoke

it's over, it said

What? I asked

Your time here

What about the wheelchairs,

the commodes, the rollators?

Who's going to replenish the

toilet paper in the bathrooms?

Don't worry about that,

it's not your concern

But...

Where the Warehouse Things Are

The clock began to tick
in my hand like some
kind of detonation device

You have nothing more to
prove here

Put down the Allen wrench, the
impact driver, the screwdriver,
the box cutter...let them go

What about my coworkers?

They are where they're
supposed to be

and you have nothing more to prove

I put down my tools as the
clock ticked

Now pick up your pen,

the clock said, that's what

you came here with when you

started

Go out and

do what you were meant to do

Be a witness...testify

I put the

clock back up on

the wall and it ticked as it

was supposed to

I walked out of

the warehouse

With a pen

and nothing more to prove

Acknowledgments

Thank you to the warehouse crew at Care Solutions Mobility Center in Hendersonville, NC: Kaye Tefel, John Hornsby, David Segal, Scott Hricsina, Annette Martin, John Suskey, James Rodriguez, Joe Ejefor, Rob Barry, Steve Jones, Gloria Foster, Sheila Culligan, Shirley Knight, Jasmine Shelton, Payton Grant and Jackson Cartner. Much appreciation to Patty Thompson and Robert Canipe of Redhawk Publications. Gratitude to Agape World Outreach in Hendersonville. Love to my mother for her constant support and to my stepfather Pete Mayberry. Appreciation to Beverly Parayno and to the Manilatown Heritage Foundation. Special thanks to Jen Soriano, Richard Jackson, Oscar Penaranda and Ron Rash. Love and remembrance to the late Crystal Cauley, poet of Hendersonville whose voice will continue to live on and inspire.

About the Author

Tony Robles is the author of the poetry collections *Cool Don't Live Here No More—A Letter to San Francisco*, *Fingerprints of a Hunger Strike,* and *Thrift Store Metamorphosis.* He was named the Carl Sandburg Writer in Residence by the Friends of Carl Sandburg in Flat Rock, NC, in 2020. He was short list nominated for Poet Laureate of San Francisco in 2017. His poetry, short stories, and essays have appeared in numerous publications. He earned his MFA in creative writing from Vermont College of Fine Arts in 2023 and is currently a professor of creative writing in the MFA graduate program at Lenoir Rhyne University in North Carolina.

Made in the USA
Middletown, DE
05 September 2024

59836092R00084